# Mind Over Matter – Blisscipline Progra

## Marie R Gould

ISBN: 5849773

ISBN-13: 978-1519164971

## DEDICATION

**This is dedicated to Peter and Heather Lewis – a shining example of how to lead a full, loving and happy life.**

**It was a privilege to have known and loved you for so long – your legacy is burning bright.**

# ACKNOWLEDGEMENTS

I would like to thank <u>everyone</u> who has been involved in helping me write this programme and bring it to print. Whether that has involved providing physical help or emotional support.

I would like to thank my wonderful Mum. Thank you for bringing me into the World, for your continued love and support as well as for just being you; I truly do not know what I would do without you! Being a parent is the hardest job in the World, without any training and sometimes little support. You did not do a bad job by the looks of things.

To my gorgeous children – Rhianne and James. I gave you both life but you have given me a reason to live, and so much more. I love you to the Moon and back and obviously always will. "A daughter is the best friend you can ever have" and My Son – the man who decided to love me – for exactly who I am. You have both taught me so much.
STAY SAFE! - BE HAPPY! – ALWAYS!

Special thanks to my dear friend from School, Cass: no you were not the bully! To Sammy, for being such a brilliant guinea pig. And to Miss Lizzie and Miss Linda; for minimising the risk of ridicule.

Thanks to all my wonderful clients and mentees - new and old - for believing in me and motivating me and giving me purpose.

Finally thanks to all those that give value and have inspired, taught and motivated me, as well as my Guardian Angel(s) - you know who you are!

And to all those that have come into my life to teach me a lesson – thanks for the memories and for making me stronger and aiding my development

**Forward**

As a child I was exceptionally shy and did not perceive myself to be that attractive or worthy. Worthy of what you may ask? Looking back perhaps of love, happiness and support? This may have been my perceptions or actual facts stemming from my environment. I am not sure I truly know. It was not until later in life, that I realised just how shy, unattractive or unworthy I had felt and how this had impacted my life.

I didn't know my dad or his side of the family and my dear stepdad, with his own problems, was taken from us when I was only 15. I have since met my dad, aunty and cousins.

I was brought up by an extremely loving mum, who had to cope with so much in her life that manifested in a tremendous amount of worry and fear. No one worked as hard as my mum, and she is still working part time at the age of 69. I never doubted her love for me, but she was always worried about the future and was often very tired. My Mum owned and managed pubs during my teenage years, and this was a fun but strange way of life. If anything she was overprotective. She lost her parents very young and had limited support. As a single mum, she held down three jobs to ensure I did not miss out and she could feed us. If somebody praised me to her face, or in front of her, the common reaction was "Not my Marie", this was probably born out of the way she was brought up and through embarrassment rather than denial. Part of British culture, I wonder? Despite her situation and fears, she has never let me down though, and has always been there when I have needed her; whether a cuddle, advice or physical support (including a foggy drive to France!).
I just did not always recognise this. God Bless my Mum!

I was also very close to my wonderful Grandad but he was taken from me at the age of nine.

So the World had already taught me, by the tender age of 15, that the men in my life do not hang around – for a variety of reasons.

I was bullied at primary school; I think looking back because I was soft and an easy target, and this knocked my confidence. At a young age I remember teachers ridiculing me, in front of others, because my work was messy or I had forgotten my times tables. I went to a private secondary school, run by nuns, and had some fantastic times and friends, but often got bullied externally by youths from other schools. Upon leaving college, I found success in my working life but craved to be settled down and part of a 'normal' stable and loving family.

I felt so alone and unsupported for most of the time. My mum was always working or too tired and you don't appreciate your mum as a teenager, do you? My stepdad's death was very traumatic and not sure I really dealt with it until later in life. Being the only child of an only child was a lonely place to be. Fortune tellers and horoscopes formed a huge part of my life because they gave me 'guidance' and a belief that I would be happy in the future. My self-esteem was low and I battled with my weight. Although looking back I was a healthy size 10 to 12 and had nothing really to worry about. I craved a large loving support network to help me stick up for myself, make me feel wanted and protect me from the bullies.

Unfortunately, I continued to attract a range of bullies - some disguised as friends. I was very needy and also saw the start of anxiety problems as a teenager. I hated conflict and was scared if I conveyed how I felt, they would up and leave.

Then I met and fell in love with a younger man when I was 23, after a whirlwind romance he moved in, we were engaged, then married and then before our first wedding anniversary, pregnant with our first child – our beautiful daughter Rhianne. I found the love and security I had been craving for years and was very happy. I qualified as a teacher, my husband set up his own business, and then our darling son, James, followed a couple years later. My life should have been complete. But it wasn't.

Unfortunately, cracks were beginning to show, we were very successful on paper, but probably had not allowed enough time to get to know each other properly and the financial pressures we put ourselves under, took its toll. We looked upon material gains as the secret to happiness, instead of what was already in front of us. We moved to France, for a fresh start and better way of life, but it was not meant to be, and despite trying for the sake of the children, we eventually separated. So I came back to the UK a couple years later and started again, as a single mum.

I attracted a string of unsuitable admirers who probably resembled my Ex! Or was it a self-fulfilling prophecy I had held that 'all men leave you in the end?' I remember my mother in law saying "you need to toughen up, Marie." But why could I not be nice?

Work again was demanding yet rewarding and ensured my children did not lose out. Working full time, whilst studying part time for a degree, coupled with constant threats of redundancy – ultimately took its toll and I started to go dizzy on a regular basis. My balance was shot to pieces and the doctors kept telling me it was 'just' stress and to take some time out.

Mmm easy for them to say and the lack of control (as I was a complete control freak) was adding to the problems. To cut a very long boring story short, my fears turned my dizziness into stress related anxiety attacks and I was only fine when at home. No one told me that stress could manifest into such physical problems. I was consumed with fear. I consulted several authorities such as cognitive behaviour therapists, chiropractors and acupuncture. This remedied my balance, in the short term, but the horrible strange feelings in my head, chest and throat kept on happening. I was told on several occasions that until I left my job I would never get right. Now like that helped my situation!!

These balance problems did coincide with meeting my real dad and the acupuncturist did wonder if this had contributed to it. My body was expressing that my life was suddenly out of balance, as I finally had two parents, but had got used to just the one. The acupuncturist had only seen one other case of my problems and his patient had just met her biological father. My dear Uncle also sadly passed away from cancer (he was only 66!) around this time. Also being a single mum does mean that at times, I felt that I had the weight of the world on my shoulders, due to having all the responsibility to get it right. I believe it was a combination of things and my body was telling me, I could not proceed as I was.

Anyway, I digress - I studied, read everything I could on stress related anxiety and gradually got 99% better and am still in the job with a couple of promotions to boot! I still encountered moments especially when tired or hormonal but understanding what was happening, meant it got easier to manage. I was determined it would not beat me and it has not. Hypnotherapy helped a great deal as that subconsciously turned off the part of my brain that was pattern matching (please research amygdala for full explanation) to previous events and places where I had felt fearful and causing the regular occurrences of heightened adrenaline leading to panic attacks.

At one of my first sessions my hypnotherapist asked "when was the last time you were happy?" I honestly could not remember and if the truth be told, I had led a quite charmed life! Stress related anxiety takes over your life and makes you think irrationally, so she was trying to reframe my thinking.

I also discovered Sue Stone and managed to secure her six month positivity programme for a fraction of the cost through Groupon. Although, at full cost, it was probably still a bargain! I repeatedly read and listened to her book "Love Life, Live Life". This daily injection of positivity and daily tips really turned my life around.

I submerged myself into an "I can" rather than an "I can't" type of person. I read everything I could on relevant subjects and watched and listened to all the videos that I could get my hands on. I stopped phoning fortune tellers and reading my stars, because I now realised that I was the creator of my life and that my happiness lay in my hands only. I found myself deliriously happy on lots of different occasions and on a regular basis, even just sitting eating breakfast at my dining room table could bring a huge smile to my face. I had reframed my thoughts, had started to realise and appreciate how blessed I was, and now could experience happiness in the most simplest of situations.

However, what I discovered then was that I was beginning to become happier staying in, listening to self help and meditation audios and being alone. I do believe that this was something I needed to go through. I needed to find myself again, learn to love and appreciate me, and be happy in my own company, so I was not dependent on others. The next step was to go out there and truly live emerging like a Phoenix from the ashes. Carl Harvey and his big life self help programme and philosophy really helped me. So I cut back on my reading and listening to all these self help videos and started applying and living My Own Big Life.

Although on reflection I was allowing myself precious ME time and although I love my significant others to the moon and back, and I'm a very social person; I do enjoy time out and time alone

Anxiety was probably the most frightening thing to ever happen to me, but also the best experience that I could ever have encountered, because it really made me take responsibility and turned my life around. I stopped existing and started living. Kelly Clarkson's song "what doesn't kill you makes you stronger" really comes to mind! I had experienced bad times and hit rock bottom, but I had learnt and grown and was going to move forward, a stronger, more confident, independent and happy version of me. I had turned the anxiety into a positive.

Throughout this journey I have learnt to love myself, because until you learn to do that, no one else stands a chance. I have a photograph of me, as a beautiful little innocent girl on my chest of drawers. Every day I stop and smile and tell her that I love her very much. I just looked so innocent, safe and happy, in this photo, so it needed to take pride of place in my bedroom. It was taken on the sofa in my first home and I can remember being there with my mum and Grandad. Lots of happy memories; laughing, feeling loved and safe. Looking at this little girl brings up so much love within me.

I now often look in the mirror and think how beautiful and blessed I am.

Lost some *friends* along the way for a variety of reasons; at different stages in our development, differing values, or no longer on the same wavelength. Also through my self development work, I have managed to naturally repel the bullies. My mind and body recognises when I am being bullied and just physically and mentally won't allow it to happen. It's important to honour my feelings and do what is best for me, whilst having sympathy and forgiveness for others.

I won't judge those that like to play the victim and relish in moaning, but really don't want to do anything about it. I am not living their life. They are obviously not ready to change. However, I try to limit my exposure to "Moodhoovers" whilst wishing them all the very best. My time and energy are very precious, so I like to spend it with people who appreciate me, and want the best for me.
Also I want to spend my spare time with the people who sincerely deserve my love and support, and are wonderful company and enhance my life.

Lots of my good friends and acquaintances, when they listen to what I have to say, say to me "but that's not realistic." For example, when I say they can attract and earn more money, they are entitled to a stress free life, or they can lose weight simply and easily- just by changing their mindset.

What is reality?

Who decides what is realistic? Andy Shaw and his bug free mind programme states that "Reality is just an illusion" The great thing I have discovered is that I choose and subsequently make my own reality. My son once said "who decided which plants were weeds, and which words were swear words?" Out of the mouths of babes! He makes a very good point.

We live and are part of an abundant universe and we are actually the creators of our own lives.

The exciting thing is - we are all one energy and we are linked and are the creators of our life, and we are meant to live loving and abundant lives and truly make a difference.

I was fed up with existing and wanted to live my life to the full, so I did something about it. It is so scary stepping out of your comfort zone - but so so worth it.

Do you want the same?

Are you ready to take your first step on this wonderful journey and learn how to lead a blissful life?

I sincerely hope so!

**I love this quote (author unknown)**

**"You are braver than you believe**

**You are stronger than you seem**

**You are smarter than you think"**

**Food for thought**

This programme is not only the foundation and key for individuals to lead a happy and fulfilling personal life but can be utilised for their professional life, or particular areas of their working environment.

It can also be adapted and utilised within the corporate world. It is a solutions orientated programme. Too much time is invested in 'the problem' and if this is where energy is directed then you can get more of the same!

I love the quote by Albert Einstein "We *cannot solve our problems with the same thinking we used when we created them!*"

People often fail because they keep implementing the same solutions. Sometimes you have to find a new strategy and way of working. Although that can be scary as humans tend to be creatures of habit even if they are bad and non productive habits. We all get used to a comfy pair of slippers and their familiarity.

One of my visions for life, apart from introducing a positive newspaper and news channel, is to see the end to corporate bullying. I would love to train a diverse range of senior managers to truly respect and value their greatest resource – their internal customers. I cannot wait until the day my programme is introduced as part of management training schemes. I know the time invested will reap huge rewards; not only a happy culture but increase in productivity and profits. Massive shout out for those that already embed such a philosophy

I admire Richard Branson's outcome on life especially his attitude towards his staff. This quote, of his, really resonates with me *"Clients do not come first. Employees come first. If you take care of your employees, they will take care of the clients."* To me this is not rocket science but something that nationally top management seemingly fail to realise and more importantly develop as their culture. To me it is really short sighted and not cost effective.

Also one of my greatest achievements will be the day I see this introduced as part of our educational curriculum, so future generations get it right from the start and we reduce stress and anxieties of childhood – especially the teens. We show our children that the World is truly their oyster and build up their confidence and self-esteem bank with a range of positive experiences and beliefs.

I love this snippet from John Lennon's childhood and remember I am a teacher! *"When I was five years old my mother always told me that happiness was the key to life. When I went to school they asked me what I wanted to be when I grew up. I wrote down happy. They told me I did not understand the assignment. I told them that they did not understand life!"* RIP John – you did understand life, so sorry yours was cut short and after everything you gave to us.

The more of us that choose to adopt this way of life, the nearer we are to achieving a World Peace. We cannot change the World without changing ourselves first. It starts on the inside! Now I know it is difficult to put this fabulous book down, but you really need to go and listen to Michael Jackson's 'Man in the Mirror.' Are you emotional? Gets me every time! I would love to be able to ask him what he was thinking when he sang it.

So you can just skim this book, or read it thoroughly and take time out to complete the exercises and reflect. I sincerely hope you read it time and time again and it makes a huge difference to your life and you start to lead a truly blissful existence.

But by just taking the time to read it once, I hope it makes you smile and you introduce some positive yet simple changes into your life. Remember not having enough time is always an excuse. We can all find an extra 30 minutes a day to work on ourselves and to be honest the time taken will see huge beneficial results. Stop watching endless TV. Get up 30 minutes early. Get off social networking for just half an hour. Studies show, and Brendon Burchard made me realise, that by not checking into other people's lives and agendas for the first 30 – 60 minutes of the day, then you have time to spend on your day and goals, and this makes you 30% more productive!

Remember if your life is dictated by your electronic devices - answering emails and trawling through Facebook and Twitter – you are just reacting to the lives of others. Do you not owe it to yourself and your loved ones, to react to your own life and make time for you? Simple yet powerful.

Repetition is the key. You really need to make this a way of life, without beating yourself up if you fall off the wagon. Hence naming it my Blisscipline programme. It's not meant to be a chore but a way of life. If you do not enjoy something then there really is no point in doing it. Now that is a waste of your time.

Obviously if you want more one-to-one or group support then I am available for individual coaching or contact me to know about forthcoming workshops in your area.

Some of you may have had some exceptionally tough times and need to dig a little deeper and get some additional specialised support. I hope you discover this as soon as you can and it really is effective

My groups get huge support from each other and their progress. It also allows me to continually develop.

My website is **www.northdevonlifecoach.wix.com/mindovermatter**

I will leave you with another pearl of wisdom from Andy Shaw (creator of Bug Free Mind) "Just remember though – knowledge can be dangerous. Sometimes we think we know something, and that is enough, but we need to start applying it!" I now re-read good books and listen to awesome videos again. It is surprising what you miss or do not take in the first time round.

I often like posts on social media and find myself saying "How true is that?" and then find myself doing or saying the exact opposite. So we may agree with something and know it is true but it is time to take action and do something about it. We need to apply it to our life. We need a strategy and mine is my #Blisscipline programme. I sincerely wish it works for you too.

Oh and I would purchase a notebook, some Q cards and some nice pens.

Although I have produced this programme in a format that should allow you to take notes and scribble all over.

**Overview**

Happiness is an inside job and only you can make you happy! Simples!

As the wonderfully inspiring Katie Piper puts it *"When you accept responsibility for your choices in life, you will find your power within and realise how much control you have over your own happiness"*

So the first thing I'm going to ask you to do is make a pledge today, right here right now, that you are going to take full responsibility for your life and the results that happen. You're going to stop blaming others, the environment, and your experiences and so on.

Write this down or change it slightly if don't feel comfortable with the words

if you do not feel that you can do this, then that is fine. Perhaps reflect on why you cannot. Read some more and come back to it when you are ready.

**I (full name)**

**Declare from today (today's date)**

**Take full responsibility for my life and the results I am receiving**

**Signed**

Now there's something you really need to know at this point, excuse me for assuming you don't, if you actually do! By the way there is probably a more scientific way to explain this, but this works for me – so hope it does for you too!

We possess two minds; one being our conscious and I refer to this as our thinking mind.

The other being our subconscious, which is, in effect, a super human computer. The third element, in the mix, is what some people call our Ego, but I prefer to call it "Chimpee". Totally separate entity that causes an awful lot of trouble!

We also live by a set of values. These tend to be ingrained within us. If we are with somebody or operate within an environment, that happens not to be aligned with our set of values, then we normally find that we are not happy or content.

Your values are the things that you believe are important in the way you live and work. According to mindtools.com (2015) *"They (should) determine your priorities, and, deep down, they are probably the measures you use to tell you if your life is turning out the way you want it to!"*

How do we clarify our values? Usually we can do this, by looking at and reflecting on the "things," that make us the most happy or most upset. One of my top values is fairness and whenever I observe/witness unfairness, and then it makes me very angry and frustrated.

From the following list and please feel free to add any – choose 10 - 20 that really resonate with you

| | | | |
|---|---|---|---|
| Accountability | Dependability | Helpful | Reliability |
| Accuracy | Determination | Honesty | Resourcefulness |
| Achievement | Diligence | Honour | Restraint |
| Adventure | Discipline | Humility | Rigour |
| Altruism | Discretion | Independence | Security |
| Ambition | Diversity | Ingenuity | Self-actualisation |
| Assertiveness | Dynamism | Integrity | Self-control |
| Balance | Economical | Intuitiveness | Selflessness |
| Belonging | Effectiveness | Insightfulness | Self-reliance |
| Boldness | Efficiency | Intelligence | Sensitivity |
| Bliss | Elegance | Intellect | Serenity |
| Calm | Empathy | Intuition | Service |
| Carefulness | Enjoyment | Joy | Shrewdness |
| Challenge | Enthusiasm | Justice | Simplicity |
| Cheerfulness | Equality | Leadership | Speed |
| Clarity | Excellence | Legacy | Spontaneity |
| Commitment | Excitement | Love | Stability |
| Community | Exploration | Loyalty | Strategic |
| Compassion | Expressiveness | Making a difference | Strength |
| Competitiveness | Fairness | Mastery | Structure |
| Compliance | Faith | Obedience | Success |
| Conscientious | Faithfulness | Openness | Support |
| Consistency | Family | Order | Teamwork |
| Contentment | Fitness | Originality | Thankfulness |
| Continual improvement | Fluency | Patience | Thoroughness |
| Contribution | Focus | Patriotism | Thoughtfulness |
| Control | Freedom | Perfection | Tolerance |
| Cooperation | Fun | Piety | Trustworthiness |
| Correctness | Generosity | Positivity | Understanding |
| Courtesy | Goodness | Practicality | Uniqueness |
| Creativity | Grace | Preparedness | Unity |
| Curiosity | Growth | Professionalism | Usefulness |
| Decisiveness | Happiness | Prudence | Vision |
| Democracy | Health | Quality | Vitality |

Write these on a separate sheet of paper

Take two at a time and ask yourself "If I could only satisfy one of these, which one would I choose?"

You should come up with your top 5 – 10    Take some time on this, as you are starting to dig deep

The exercise and video found on www.mindtools.com, may be worth a read.


Once you have clearly defined your values and perhaps come up with your top five then it is time to ascertain your happiness levels within specific areas of your life. You could change this to areas of your business or elements of your team

**My Top Values are:**

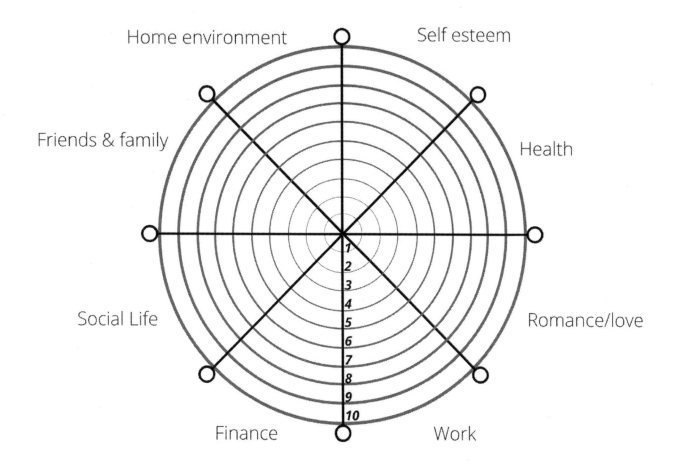

Above is quite a generic Wheel of Life. You can change the titles of each of the sections if they don't match your life.

Within each of the sections - colour in - to your current level of satisfaction.

10 being highly satisfied, 1 being unsatisfied.

Your wheel should balance!

If it's wobbly, then the areas you scored the lowest are the areas you need to look at one by one.

Now I'd like you to take some time to carry out the following activity as well - using your lovely notepad and pens, write down in glorified detail what each of your areas would look like if you were at a 10

Also do your goals and overall intentions (10's) align with your values, significant others and your environment?

Any surprises?

Now what you really need to know is that this takes repetition and is a way of life.

We need to stick at it, but you are only human so please don't beat yourself up if you fall off the wagon now and again.

Hence calling it my #Blisscipline programme

I apologise to all the quantum-physicists out there and probably most religious leaders but what you really truly need to know is that we are all made up of the same energy; ourselves, the bed we lie in, the car we drive, the humans that we share this world with, to the glass of wine you end your hectic day with.

We are all actually magnets and the energy we send out we attract back

Have you ever thought something like "I might buy a yellow car" and then suddenly everywhere you go yellow cars appear?

I am a great believer in the Law of Attraction or as some people would say the Law of Awareness. "The Secret" is a great read and watch.

Simply put:-

- What we think - we create

- What we feel - we attract

- What we imagine - we become

However, I do feel that we need to take inspired action along the way. Especially as and when the universe gives us the relevant opportunities

**Step one.  TRAINING YOUR CONSCIOUS MIND TO BE AN ASSET**

Henry Ford was a really successful man and no doubt his wonderful mantra *"Whether you think you can or you can't, you're right"* helped him a great deal.  This is so simple yet so true and powerful.

**Our thoughts control the outcomes we see manifest in our lives!**

Now re-read that again and again!

**Our thoughts control the outcomes we see manifest in our lives!**

We have approximately 90000 thoughts per day and 60000 are repetitive!

What are your most dominant thoughts?

Are they positive and useful or negative and not?

Or a mixture?  Or does it depend on what is going on around you, how much sleep you have managed to get and perhaps your hormones and so forth?

What first put me on track for my Blissful life was when I started to understand that it is only you who can allow thoughts to take up residence in your mind.  In a nutshell - the thoughts that you think; determine how you feel, and ultimately how you feel, influences the World around you!

Therefore, it is essential that you learn to choose your thoughts with an awareness of their power and endeavour to seed only beneficial thoughts in your mind.

It is imperative that you choose your every thought with care because the thoughts you seed in your mind, the concepts and beliefs you accept with feeling, inevitably become your own living reality.

How you choose to think today influences all your tomorrows, and your life is far too valuable not too!

Also what does your internal voice sound like?

What do you tell yourself on a regular basis?

I hope you speak to yourself as you would to someone you really love, care for and only want the best for them

Stop and have a long **think** about this (see what I did there?)

Now this is where 'Chimpee' comes into play

Some people refer to this internal voice as their Ego. It is kind of like our guardian. There just to try and protect and keep us safe and in our comfort zone. It looks out for any perceived dangers and tells us repeatedly we are not safe (inner mind chatter – monkey mind) or manifests it into physical feelings and sensations in the body.  It was extremely useful when we were cavemen; thankfully most current dangers are not so imminent and life threatening

However, our fear signals tend to be identical whether it is a hungry lion we are facing or having to participate in public speaking.

I have read somewhere that more people are more scared of public speaking than death! I can totally emphasise with that.

Our fight or flight system is still the same as it was when we were cavemen and just had to make sure that we ate, slept, reproduced and survived!  This all relates to our Amygdala; and its dictionary definition is  *"a roughly almond-shaped mass of grey matter inside each cerebral hemisphere, involved with the experiencing of emotions"*  Fear being one of our many emotions.

Fear often helps us with self-preservation. We feel fear, as well as related emotions, in order to protect ourselves from danger and to heighten our awareness. This awareness is thought to be controlled by a section of the brain known as the amygdala.  I personally believe the fact that this has not evolved, and reprogrammed itself,  to look at what constitutes real dangers in the 21st century can lead to anxiety and panic attacks in environments that do not pose real danger to us but make us extremely anxious.

Our fast pace of life with constant digital interactions definitely feeds this - in my experience at any rate.

It also has a habit of pattern matching. Exacerbating the anxieties in certain places and at certain times. Breaking this cycle is so important but it is scary.

When I was poorly I needed to make sure that I had an easy escape route to lessen the feelings. Sitting near the door in a meeting for instance. I went from having dizzy spells standing up to feeling so awful ordering a glass of pinot at the bar. Once I discovered what was happening to me -slowly but surely I started to make myself attend events and meetings and so forth. Repeatedly rationalising the situations when I was calm and visualising myself coping and smiling. I now only experience debilitating anxiety when probably I should!

It was quite a journey though. But the reverse happens with pattern matching - the more you do something and are 'OK' the more positive and productive evidence you are storing in your evidence bank (more about this in step 2) This all links to what you are thinking and what you are telling yourself - also not looking for negative evidence to back up irrational thoughts and feelings

Acknowledging that you feel stressed or threatened and that your fight or flight response has been activated is the first step. Becoming aware of how your emotions and body react to significant stress. Journaling an episode and reviewing later may help understand your responses.

Next step is to try and calm down and take control. This sounds easier then it is but with practice it does get easier. Continually remind yourself that what you are feeling is an automatic response, not necessarily the best or most logical/practical one.

When you are calm, reflect on the situation and analyse it practically and come up with a thoughtful rational solution. Becoming aware of your triggers and warning signs, and noticing when they are present. A good way is to pay attention to your breathing; this is where discovering Mindfulness really helped me.

Breathe slowly and evenly. Think about the speed and rhythm of your breaths, and focus on what's going on in your body as you inhale and exhale.

*"Follow your breathes and your thoughts will follow"*

This also helped me master my 'Chimpee'. I highly recommend you read The Chimp Paradox - if you want to learn this in more detail. I would also recommend researching amygdala and mindfulness.

We also reinforce this in further steps.

Remember what Esther Jno-Charles states *"What you focus on expands. So focus on what you want not what you do not want!"*

Your own negative thought patterns provide the energies that feed your problems and keep them alive; so you need to learn how to switch the energy around

Focus your thought energy on how you want things to be rather than how you don't want them to be and withdraw all your thought energy from your problems so that you can only attract the solutions.

You can then start attracting good fortune like a magnet!

When I was poorly all I ever did was talk about it, to anyone and everyone that would listen. So guess what it kept happening because that is where my energies lay. When I finally knew what I, and 'Chimpee' was saying was not true; I needed to knock him out for a bit – I found hypnotherapy a huge help.

I do try and master my 'Chimpee' by looking upon him as a very well meaningful yet inexperienced friend. I try to talk to him (yes mine is male) as I would a real person. Understanding what he is trying to do, being gentle with him. I often have to 'exercise my Chimpee' with a supportive and understanding friend - when I have 'Chimpee Mind' say for example when someone has rattled my unfairness value.

We look more in depth, in later steps, at how others around us can influence our thoughts and feelings. I have become very attuned to the language others may use and how unhelpful it can be. I learnt very soon, though, it's not always best to point it out as not everyone is ready to change.

**Can you recognise any of these?**

**"I can't afford it"** well guess what you never will

**"Why does it always happen to me?"**

**"That's out of my reach"**

**"That's just not realistic"**

**"Life's unfair"**

**"I am always ill"**

Try not to let the negativity of others to seep into your thinking patterns and drain your positive energy.

My internal mind chatter was quite negative and self-destructive and I needed to change that.

Also I needed to recognise when I was using my human mind or when "Chimpee" was sticking his oar in.

Remember:

Logical and rational thinking – Human

Emotional and irrational – Good old 'Chimpee'

Writing out a list of positive affirmations, sticking them everywhere, as well as repeating them truly helped in the beginning.

Also listening regularly to positive audios; such as guided meditations for relaxation and most definitely confidence building, and self esteem building ones.

The best overarching affirmations I found to be most effective are:

# I AM POWERFUL

# I AM STRONG

# I AM LOVING

# I AM COMPLETE

# I AM HAPPY

# I AM HARMONIOUS

# I AM HEALTHY

# I AM ABUNDANT

Do these work for you ?

You may want to adapt for different situations.

You will get more proficient as you go and use ones that feel right to you and your situation.

Keeping a thought diary helps, or if you have a good positive friend you trust, ask them to take note of your everyday language.

Ask yourself – "What am I thinking now?"  Or "What am I feeling now?"  This brings you back to the present moment.

Thinking back to your Wheel of Life and the areas where you scored low and are stuck?  Take some time to think what thoughts you have been thinking that may have resulted in these outcomes?

Sue Stone has been a huge source of inspiration to me and I found it difficult to keep track or notice my thoughts and language at the beginning of my journey. So I love her top tips that originate from Rhonda Byrne.  www.suestone.com

---

**Do not worry at all about negative thoughts and do not try to control them**

**All you have to do is begin to think good THOUGHTS each day.**

**Plant as many good thoughts as you can each day.**

**As you begin to think good thoughts you will ATTRACT more and more good thoughts and eventually the good thoughts will wipe out the negative thoughts altogether.**

---

What this made me realise was that by asking myself and others to keep a thought diary, I may be unintentionally giving too much energy to negative thoughts,  whereas Sue's method starts training you to focus on the positive and changing your negative habits.

I cannot promise that bad things won't happen, if you introduce my programme into your life. We are going to lose people along the way and this has to be processed and somehow dealt with so you can start healing. If bad things have happened to you then I am sincerely sorry.

What I have noticed since introducing #Blisscipline is that the 'bad' things are less and less - and some of the issues I perceived as 'bad' were not as bad as they seem or they could be far far far worse.  I am also more prepared when I do suffer a loss, face a challenge or time of uncertainty.

Your thoughts alone are causing your suffering. How you react to situations and your perceptions are what cause your internal feelings.

Please please please please, whatever you do, do not suppress any sad, bad or angry feelings. I'm not asking you to focus on them and let them take over your lives but you just need to be aware that you're feeling like this and quietly acknowledge them. You don't have to analyse them because again then you are giving them all your energy

We must not resist bad thoughts or feelings just welcome and then be aware and not judge. This takes away their power.  And make sure you are focussing on having positive thoughts than looking out too much for the baddies.

Use the bad thoughts and anger as fuel for making positive changes.

Also be very aware of your thoughts towards other people and how they treat you. You do not live their lives so you cannot judge them. If someone treats you bad it is because they have problems and nothing usually personally against you.  It is a reflection of their inner turmoil. Forgive them, forget them and move on. Remember, what you give is what you receive. I am a great believer in Karma.

I found asking myself "How come I?" Questions really helped. "How come I earn so much money?" "How come I am so beautiful?". My best friend and I had some real fun with this when we discovered it. Although the "how can we drink so much wine and not get hungover?" is probably not very good recommendation

Stress comes about from you, 'Chimpee' and maybe others, constantly telling you that "you have too much to do", "you cannot cope", and/or "you do not have enough time to complete everything" and so on.  It also stems from your fears and anxieties

What if I try and I fail?

One way to ascertain what you're thinking is how you are feeling. Your thoughts create your feelings. It is never the actual situation or experience that makes you feel happy or sad or angry, but your thoughts about the situation!    **Your thoughts are not facts**

| | |
|---|---|
| **The next time you are stressed - ask yourself:** | |
| "What problems do I actually have right here, right now? | |
| "What am I saying to myself to result in this?" | |
| **Some other useful actions to take** | |
| Keep a thought diary - it does get easier | |
| Sue Stone's Top Tip - replace with positive | |
| Quiet Time and MIndfulness - give yourself permission for more ME time | |
| Watch out for "Chimpee" and your internal mind chatter | |
| Focus on what you want not what you do not | |
| **Ask yourself:** | |
| "Is there a blessing/silver lining in this situation" | |
| "What am I thinking/feeling right now?" | |
| "How come I.......................................... " questions | |
| "What's my next thought?" | |

## Step two. REFORMATTING YOUR SUBCONSCIOUS MIND

Now this is where it starts to get even more exciting if not rather scary. Our subconscious mind is like a super human computer and it does everything the conscious mind instructs it too. Just like my children, NOT ●

It is made up from a bunch of evidence we have picked up and stored along the way. Between the ages of 2 and 6 we form a range of ingrained beliefs that are hard to shift. We get these from the important people in our lives as well as our experiences. Then as we got older we started to add more and more.

When our conscious mind needs to make a decision then we turn to this computer without knowing for advice as to what happened before. Unfortunately "Chimpee" is quick and gets their first and starts putting doubts, concerns, fears and worries into our mind.

If any area of your life is stuck or not going to plan, then you will have limiting beliefs that are affecting this. Look back and reflect on your Wheel of Life. Which areas are not completely satisfying you, what are your related beliefs?

Sometimes if you continue to be stuck and things won't improve despite you trying to shift, your subconscious may be trying to teach you a valuable lesson. Patience, letting go and so on.

Your subconscious can be reformatted but takes time and repetition

Being aware of your limiting beliefs and bringing them to the surface is a great start. Acknowledge them, rather than resist and you start taking their power away.

Remember, if you have negative limiting beliefs then you won't manifest what you desire.

Once you start becoming aware of them then they're easier to shift.

It is worth noting that the subconscious does not recognise the negative so changing a limiting belief about your weight To "I am not fat" just isn't going to work. Try "I am the correct healthy weight for me"

Positive affirmations do not work alone but are a good start. Once you have completed the following activity – write a set of relevant positive affirmations and stick them on post its, repeat on a regular basis, keep writing them down and perhaps even record yourself saying them and keep listening. I used to find repeating them whilst driving was very productive.

You may want to work on this over a period of time but I suggest you write down what first comes to mind.

So write down your Top Ten limiting beliefs for example; life's a struggle, life's unfair, I am fat, you have to work hard for a living, I am always skint, there are no decent men/women, I am useless, I am clumsy and so on.

1

2

3

4

5

6

7

8

9

10

Choose the one(s) you want to start working on and change into a positive affirmation. Money flows easily into my life perhaps?

Ask yourself the following:

Is it possible?

How much do you want this 10/10?

Is it in your control?

Then keep repeating it. It may feel strange to start with, but with repetition then it will work,

Also, look for evidence – inspiring and relevant news stories or think of people you know who have already achieved it. Also, look to your past achievements as proof.

Research has shown that you can usually place your limiting beliefs into three categories

- **If I try I will fail**

- **I am not worthy**

- **No one will want me**

Have a go at placing your limiting beliefs into these categories.  What does it say about you?

Again revert back to your Wheel of Life – what limiting beliefs do you possess that are keeping you stuck in some areas and more importantly what supportive beliefs are ensuring you are successful in others?

Lisa Nichols, star of The Secret, is another inspiration of mine. She has an amazing guided meditation about your worthiness.  Also, she gets you to complete a similar exercise where you write down all your limiting beliefs in a notepad and leave four lines between them. Read them out and then go back and cross out and replace, with a red pen, a positive replacement.

We are creatures of habits but we can break our bad habits and with regular repetition and focus.

Also you may want to reflect on the consequences of not transforming these limiting beliefs.

What will you be missing out on?

How will it make you feel?

Are you setting a good example for your significant others, especially your children?

Do you want to get to old age and regret the things you did not do?

Life is not a dress rehearsal!

**Step three. GOOD VIBRATIONS**

What you think and what you believe (Steps one and two) impacts on what we feel and, in turn, then becomes the outcomes and results we see manifesting in our lives

**Feeling** happy is a lot more powerful than just saying, thinking and repeating you are happy

Now I know when you're feeling down and life is throwing you lemons, it's difficult to get out of that spiral and feel happy about anything. But it is very important to learn how to move into a more positive energy and feel and transmit much more productive vibrations. You know the saying 'I am in a right state!'? Well I want you to be in THE RIGHT state (of mind)

If the only one thing that you take out from reading this book is the following tip, I will be very grateful. Be grateful for what you have in life, and I mean the small things as well as the big things: the smile from your children or even a stranger in a queue, the parking space where and when you needed it, the sunshine, and the rain to do its thing and so on.

Keeping a gratitude book turned my life around. I do this every morning and evening whenever possible. I also say thank you a lot for all the good things that come my way. The impromptu hug from one of my children, the bargains I find in the supermarket, the reduced hotel deal, the helping hand from one of my colleagues and so on. This starts changing your life and getting you to truly appreciate everything you have in your life already. When you start realising and appreciating all the good in your life, then you start attracting more abundance. If you sit around moaning about your lack of money or your bad job, your selfish friends, then guess what you attract more of the same.

As the wise quote by Maltbie D. Babcock points out *"Better to lose count while naming your* **blessings** *than to lose your blessing to counting your troubles!"*

I have truly found then when Gratitude appears Fear disappears!

So we need to find ways to regularly experience the following good vibrations:

**Love**

**Peace**

**Calm**

**Contentment**

**Enjoyment**

**Gratitude**

Again what you think, feel and how you act, is what you and your life reflects

You need to find a way to ensure you are living in a positive vibrational state for as much of your life as you possibly can.

Experiencing ME time really helps

During a recent workshop many of my clients said when they had started feeling bad, sad and down, they found it really useful to start writing their gratitude list again on a daily basis. I pointed out that perhaps if they had not stopped writing it, in the first place, they may have not begun to feel so down!

Making a list of things, people, places, and experiences that you are grateful for, starts reprogramming both your minds. You start thinking more happy thoughts and you place productive evidence into that super human computer of yours that in turn become beliefs. You are focusing on the good rather than the bad and guess what – you start attracting more of this good stuff.

Mediation and paraliminals are great, as well as mindfulness and breathing techniques. Oh and throw in regular massages and heaven comes to mind. Go on spoil yourself, you work hard, you deserve it and the results will be immense.

I also love getting lost in a really good book or even trashy novel. It makes me switch off. I now do not wait until my holidays to do this either.

I find gardening and walks in the countryside really help ground me. When was the last time you went for a walk and truly noticed all of the abundance around us? Not just the sun in the sky, or the air that we breathe but also the trees and the bushes. Butterflies and honeysuckle really do it for me.

I am also very luck to live near the sea (although I do not always appreciate it as much as I should) but there is something about walking on the beach and listening to the water that really calms me - even on a freezing cold day

I have a playlist on my ipod with uplifting music that puts a big smile on my face and makes me feel happy. Sometimes I have been known to bop around the lounge - exercise and mental shift all in one. Irene Cara's 'Flashdance - What a Feeling' really says it all for me.

Sometimes a song comes on - like my wedding song - (Simply the Best by Tina Turner if you are interested) and I listen to it and reflect and remember the good times. Sometimes I shuffle onto the next one.

I have recently been given some mindfulness colouring books and I love them. Miss Always Busy And Overthinking can really stop and get lost in the moment. It takes me to a place in my childhood where I was relaxed and free

They say Laughter is the best medicine and I quite agree. Having a really good belly laugh with my significant troop really helps especially when I end up snorting loudly and crying. Sometimes I do not want company though (and that is OK) so I turn on a comedy or read a good book, or follow funny people on social media.

What makes you laugh and smile?

Creative visualisation is also a great tool. Start by closing your eyes and imagining you living your new life in Technicolor detail with appropriate sounds. These pictures and sound trick your subconscious mind into believing that they are really happening. It takes repetition and perseverance. I did find it very difficult because 'Chimpee' would start distracting me and telling me I was bored and useless at it. There is a wealth of support out there. Natalie Ledwell and her mind movies are brilliant, and there is also a wealth of guided meditations and paraliminals.

Did you have a good imagination as a child and were you told that it was not real or possible so you stopped? Well now you are an adult - you are allowed to make a moving picture in your mind; a picture of you as you see yourself having accomplished all the desired changed - the unwanted patterns of behaviour have ceased all that you want it to be is - see it - feel it - know it

Experience it ! Everything just as you want it to be!

The picture becomes clearer, brighter, bigger. The new picture dominates the screen, brilliant, beautiful, wonderful and leave the picture in the mirror of your mind to serve as an attracting force and it will

Some people find it really useful to have an actual vision board; where they collect and pin relevant pictures, items and images to it.

Now we come to what can be the tricky bit. Hopefully you are buzzing and feeling all warm inside. You can now appreciate that you can change your life and be truly happy. You are realising that you need to be happy internally rather than expect external influences to make you happy. But we are fortunate enough to share this planet with a wide range of people that mean a wealth of different things to us and all have their own personalities. So choose your troop and influences carefully, where ever possible.

I found, in the beginning, it was best not to share too much detail of my goals and plans with my friends and family. Most of them were exceptionally well meaning but could quite easily put a dampener on what I was trying to achieve. And some of our troop may have their own agenda, maybe selfish, or may not want us to change because they are scared of where they fit in.

Once they start seeing your awesome results and they realise they do still have a special part to play, then it may be easier to spill the beans. Lead by example. So as I said previously, I lost a few along the way which was very sad but very necessary, if I was going to continue to lead this happy life.

My significant troop now only includes those on the same wavelength and those that inspire, love and want the best for me. Long gone are the days where I would be bullied into submission and their way of thinking. This means both personally and professionally.

I have not turned into some selfish self-absorbed monster, but know that I need looking after and my feelings count just as much as the next persons. Hopefully I am still an amazing mother, as that is quite a unique job, but still needs boundaries.

Although I believe you need to look after number One, to allow you to look after others if there is something or someone missing in your life then you need to reflect on how you are treating others

If you want more love then love

If you want more abundance then be generous

What you give you get back – always - but maybe from a different source

I also choose my surroundings and influences carefully. I have stopped watching the news and reading newspapers. I am not filling up my super human computer with a load of negativity that 'Chimpee' can utilise against me.

Let's take a devastating Plane Crash for instance - of course it needs to be reported. However, do we report just how many planes take off and land safely every minute of the day?

I still care!

I just prefer to concentrate on all the good in the World rather than the bad, so I can help attract more of the good stuff

I still want World Peace!

I do also monitor my social media influences and activities. I also try and devote time to being positive through my many social media platforms to try and make a difference to others

I now find it really difficult to spend time with negative people, the self-confessed 'victims' in life, the ones that could win an Olympic Gold for moaning. Listening to their language gets me down and their lack of gratitude for what they actually do have! But I have learnt to forgive them and not judge, as I don't, live their lives! Oh and keep a distance - wherever possible.

In my experience those that endure 'real' pain usually just try and get on with it. In most cases they can turn their negatives into positives

I am far more attuned to the language of people – and I get so frustrated, but have learnt to shut my mouth unless they ask for help. And if they do ask for help I do everything I can to support them

As a footnote and a very important if not scary end to this step; forgiveness is very powerful if you want to move forward! You don't have to condone the behaviours but by forgiving them and thanking them for teaching you a lesson; it will allow you to heal and let go of toxic bitter energies. Improving your vibrations

Being bitter, angry and resentful is not harming the perpetrators only you and that means they are winning and still hurting you. But it is your control to stop this and not allow it to affect your wonderful future.

I believe that writing it all down in a letter (and sleeping on it) then re-reading it and then burning it - really helps me.

Not forgiving others is like wanting to hurt others but drinking the poison yourself. Feelings of bitterness, anger, regret do not align with good vibrations and the positive energy you want to envelope yourself in

Remember blaming others and situations for your current situation and feelings is not going to help. You have pledged to take 100% responsibility for turning your life around

Also I think it is also very powerful to forgive yourself too

We are human, after all, and all have made mistakes

But as long as we realise that we were wrong, and learn - then we should forgive ourselves and leave in the past

Get a picture of you as a child (a happy photo) if possible or just imagine it - smile sweetly at that innocent soul and forgive them and tell them on a regular basis that you love them - unconditionally

You may want to repeat this

Now go and find the Beach Boys famous song on spotify or youtube or........... **Good Vibrations -** have a bop and big smile on your face - be grateful for what you have learnt so far and imagine that shiny happy future that is waiting for you

Congratulate yourself at sticking with it and being Blissciplined.

**Step four. BEING PRESENT!**

The only moment you are guaranteed is right here, right now. Tomorrow may never come. So hurry up and finish this book!! If you are depressed you tend to live in the past, if you are anxious you are living in the future

I do appreciate that some people do suffer deep debilitating depression and I sincerely hope that if this applies to you - then you research and get all the help you deserve and move forward with clear strategies in place

I was always such a worry wart! With a very overactive mind. What is the point in worrying? You are just stealing your joy and focussing all your wonderful powerful energy and thoughts on things that probably never happen. Or there is a chance they will if you keep thinking and visualising them!

Worrying is like praying for what you don't want ! This is so powerful that I am going to repeat this

*Worrying is like praying for what you don't want ….*

A friend was worrying about her exam and assignment results and said to me "I'm just going to think that I failed and then I won't be disappointed!" Guess what, she failed. So when the time came for her to retake them, I had a little chat with her and her 'Chimpee'. I got her telling herself that she was brilliant and had passed and visualising the success, and guess what, she passed ●

When my anxieties start rearing their ugly heads and I'm worrying about things I can't control, I ask myself repeatedly "What problems do I have right here right now?" It's really helped me to focus, that in the current time I don't actually have any problems, and my anxiety is silly.

Smiling is a wonderful tool

As discussed in Step 3 discovering 'Mindfulness' was also a major part of my recovery process. I highly recommend introducing this as a part of your new way of life

Remember that the past and the future only exist in your mind and how you perceive it to be. I hope that's given you some real food for thought!

Perhaps your perception of your past is not factually correct. Perhaps you can start remembering it in a better light

Perhaps your perception of the past is, unfortunately, very accurate and very painful and, again, I am so sorry. Again is there more specialised help to help you move forward?

Take some time out here maybe

Letting go can be so painful yet so therapeutic

There are lots of tools and strategies to let go of anything that is holding you back

I find the 'cutting cords' exercise so very helpful

Close your eyes and think about the person or thing that is causing you pain - imagine that there are cords binding you together - with a smile on your face - wish them well and say goodbye as you cut the cords and separate you and they float away. I have found that some people need more industrial strength scissors and you may have to repeat this

Or imagine them as a large helium balloon and as you let go of the string; wish them well, say you love them, say Goodbye and thank you! This can feel rather strange to start with but it does work

You only have this moment now! So enjoy it and make the most of it. You do not have to let your past ruin your future. Make a decision that today is a new day and tomorrow a new chapter.

Also, understanding and managing my 'Chimpee' has taken time and perseverance. I keep reading The Chimp Paradox. My anxieties left me having problems driving and especially overtaking. Having these overwhelming feelings can catch me by surprise and you can imagine how dangerous this can be. I have taken to avoiding such situations as it is not like when it happened in a certain room and I could just up and leave.

The other night I was really tired and knew I had to drive on a piece of road that historically has made me have these horrible sensations. I told 'Chimpee' gently how him making me have these feelings meant that I would have to get others to drive, who may not be as good as me and I would be out of control and therefore could crash. I have never had a crash and am always safe. If he kept making me feel like this then the chances of me crashing were far more likely to happen and it would limit our fun times as we would be trapped. Guess what – I drove with confidence and enjoyment. Really was a case of Mind over Matter.

Going with the flow and being spontaneous is such a happy way to be. I would like you to think, however, that life is a game, you need a plan and some intentions, which leads us very nicely onto step five.

**Step five. DESIGN YOUR LIFE**

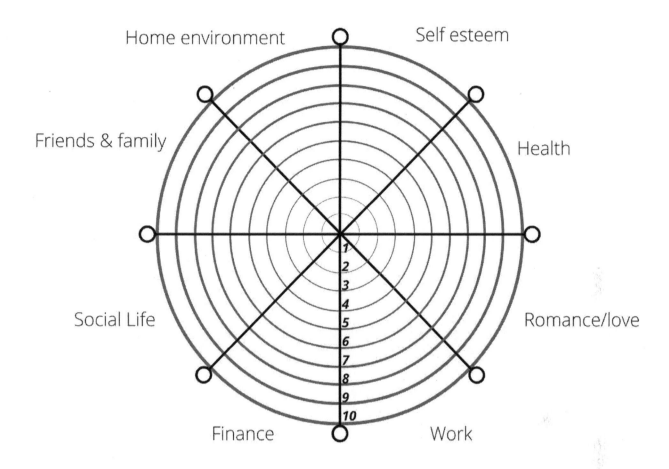

Now go and retrieve the wheel that you produced at the beginning of this book. Taking into account everything you've learnt and how you are feeling – is this wheel a true reflection of your life and your desires and most importantly is it aligned with your values.

I suggest that you undertake this exercise again.

Now I want you to take out your pad and pens and make a tick list for each separate area of your life. So if you're looking for a relationship you may want to put; he's taller than me so I can wear heels, be polite and all those important qualities that are aligned with your values as well as your desires.

Then repeat for all the other areas of your life or your goals and intentions

Taking all this into account, I want you to design your life in glorious technicolour. Remember you are the director of your life story so please make it a happy ending. If it's easier, look at me as your fairy godmother, and with my magic wand, I can grant you all your wishes.

Write down, USING THE PRESENT TENSE, how your life looks and, and more importantly how you feel. Don't leave any stone unturned and ensure every minute detail is covered.  Come back to this on a regular basis.  Then regularly visualise you living this life.  Pretend you are at the cinema watching the story of your wonderful life.

I found in the beginning, as I wanted to make lots of changes, I could not concentrate, so although I clearly knew all of my desired outcomes – I started to break them down and concentrate on the priorities and found it easier achieving them one by one.

Now many specialists will say that this is all you have to do.  But I believe a little action helps inspire and motivate us.

Remember "I want don't get".  You wanting something says to the universe there is lack in your life.  So everything is visualised and stated using the present tense and be grateful and thankful for everything you do have.

A dream of mine is to own a BMW 118i SE convertible in Valencia orange. However I am exceptionally grateful for the reliable and economic car I do own now.  Update - Since first publishing this I am now a proud owner of a spice orange mini convertible (with BMW engine) although next time will finetune my vision so it does not have to be dependent on a nasty car accident!

Also I have often set my intentions for something specific; career, relationship, pay rise but something better has turned up. The Universe does know best. What I tend to find most useful is that when I'm writing my intentions and I do this for the next month and the next year and so on, I write how I feel.

*I live in my perfect happy dream home which makes me feel safe and secure and allows me to entertain as well as finding peace and harmony*

*I am blessed with a career that not only rewards me significantly but makes me feel respected, free and in control*

Now one last thing. I want you to write a letter to your great grandchild or someone else who is very special to you.  This letter will be given to them on the day that you pass away. Tell this darling legacy of yours everything they need to know to lead a happy and full life.

Put this letter away and make a note to take it out in approximately a years' time.

This is the advice you should be giving yourself!

I wish you a very happy, fulfilling life where you live your life to the fullest and reach your full potential.  You are a very special unique person and have been put on this planet for a purpose

I hope you discover this and soon

Take care of yourself!

**Summary**

So then?

What are you thinking?

What are you feeling?

What are your next steps?

**What were your biggest lightbulb moments?**

Please please, get in touch with your success stories

Shout if you want further advice and clarification or some specific coaching

I sincerely wish you an exceptionally happy and abundant ever after

Further reading/watching

Sue Stone
Fiona Harrold
The Go Giver
The Secret
The Chimp Paradox
Ruby Wax
Carl Harvey and The Big Life
Dr Wayne Dyer's The Shift

Printed in Great Britain
by Amazon

10584679R00027